IMAGES
of America

MOREHEAD CITY
ON THE WATERFRONT

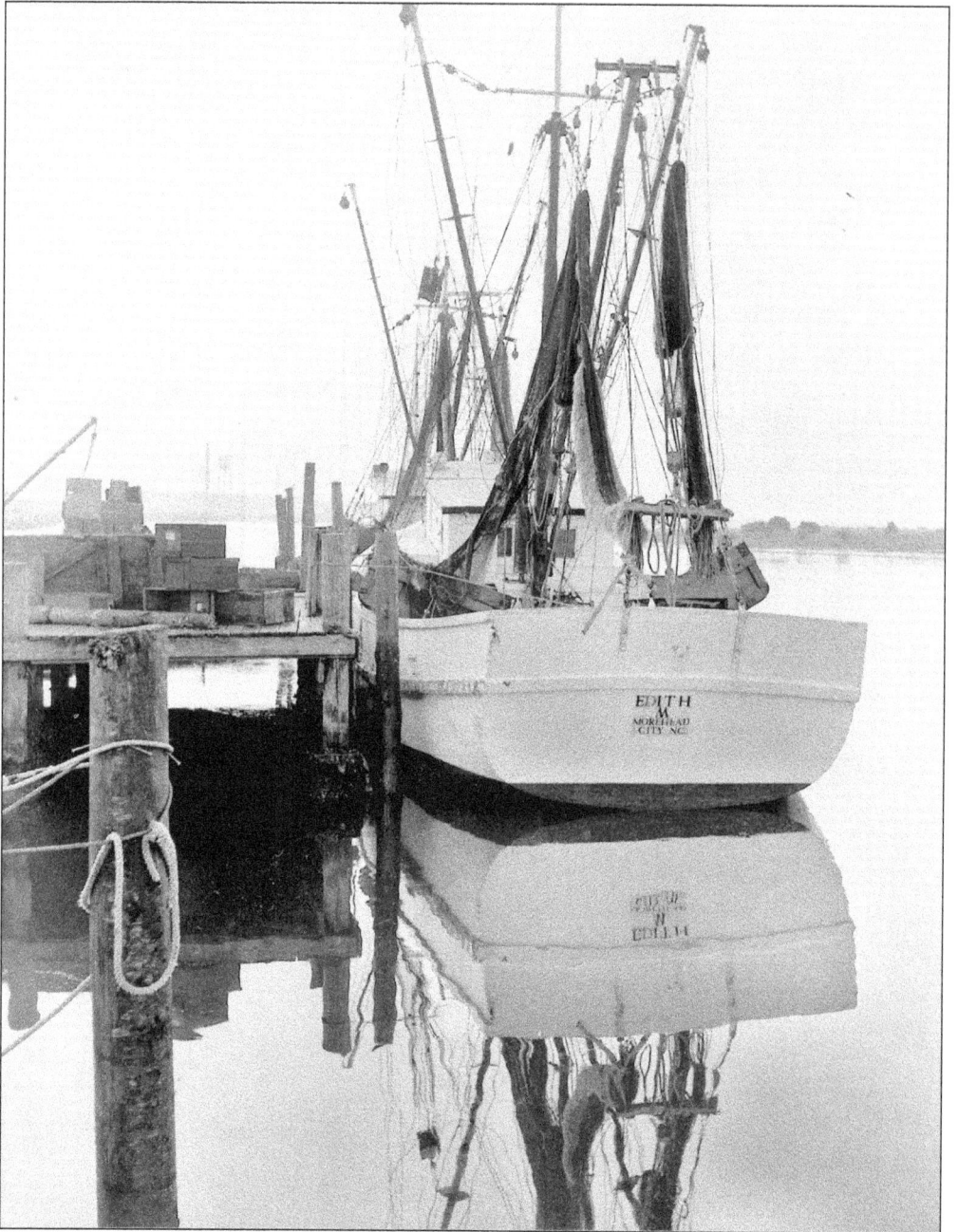

The shrimp trawler *Edith* M. is seen here at rest in the early morning calm after a night trawling for shrimp. The photo is from 1956.

IMAGES
of America

MOREHEAD CITY
ON THE WATERFRONT

Reginald Worth Lewis Jr.

ARCADIA
PUBLISHING

Published by Arcadia Publishing
Charleston, South Carolina

Library of Congress Catalog Card Number: 2004101547

For all general information contact Arcadia Publishing at:
Telephone 843-853-2070
Fax 843-853-0044
E-mail sales@arcadiapublishing.com
For customer service and orders:
Toll-Free 1-888-313-2665

Visit us on the Internet at www.arcadiapublishing.com

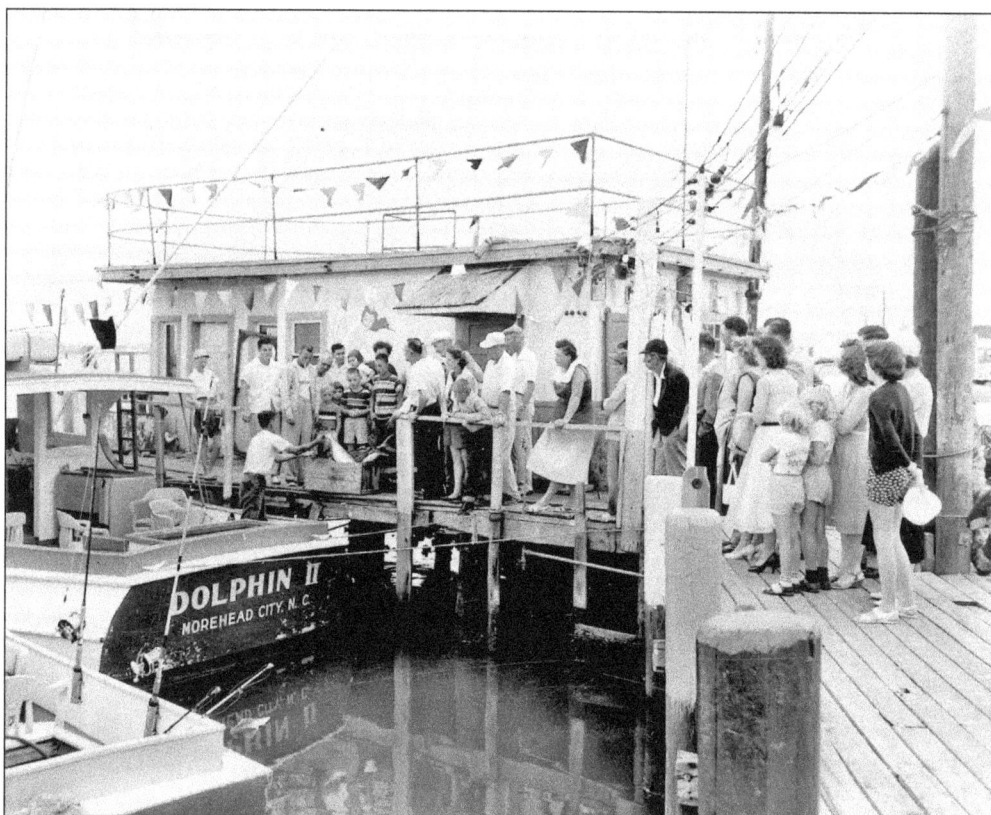

This 1952 image shows a typical scene on a summer afternoon along the Morehead City waterfront, where a crowd of visitors and locals has gathered to view the catch of the day. This was always a time of excitement and anticipation.

CONTENTS

ACKNOWLEDGMENTS

I wish to give a very special thanks to Jack Spencer Goodwin and Cindi Hamilton of the Carteret County Historical Society for their support in putting this book together. Some images used in this book are courtesy of the Carteret County Historical Society and a very grateful thank you is given for allowing the use of these images. I wish to thank Tom Hobbs for his support and the use of a Speed Graphic Graflex camera. This book would not have been possible without the assistance and encouragement of my wife, Gay Lewis, and my son, Jordan Lewis.

I feel very fortunate to be the son of a very talented photographer and artist who loved the people of Morehead City and the waterfront. There were many times while preparing this book that I wished he were still here. Thanks to his notes, records, and preservation of his negatives, he was able to be with me through his work.

There are many others who deserve thanks, but to list them all would take a book in itself. I wish to give them a special thank you; they know who they are and it was a privilege to have spoken with them.

The Morehead City waterfront is seen here as it looks today, looking west from the port. The North Carolina Seafood Festival is held along the waterfront each year on the first weekend in October.

INTRODUCTION

My fondest memories of growing up in Morehead City as the son of a waterfront artist and photographer include spending time at the fish houses, the docks, and all the other places that made the waterfront unique. It was truly an experience and a real privilege to have spent time with my father—helping him carry his cameras while he went to the fish houses, boats, restaurants, and fish racks to shoot photos.

I was fortunate as I got older to work in many of these places (back then you were able to start work at a much younger age). I remember many afternoons unloading the boats, cleaning fish, and packing the fish boxes with ice, or whatever other job they had for me to do. I would make $1 or $2 a day, and for a kid that was a lot of money. The memories were good ones.

Being around the fish house was especially good. Each one had a character of its own and really fascinating things would happen all the time. One might not think so, but even the smells of the sea and the sounds of the boat engines were exciting. I remember that a few fish houses had their own walk-in coolers with ice machines. They made ice in soft flakes—it was so good to eat. Afternoons were especially busy on the waterfront as the Lucky Seven fishing fleet and other charter boats would return from a day's fishing. Large crowds would gather on the dock and in and around the fish houses to get a glimpse of the day's catch. There were also numerous exhibits in and around Ottis's Fish House that showcased photos of previous fish catches, art carvings by local artists and fishermen of fish, birds, and other sea life, handmade wood models of boats from this area, and many other items of interest.

My father always gave a copy of his photos to the boat captains, mates, or Captain Ottis. Ottis would put them in the fish house for all to see. These displays of waterfront life drew attention from locals and tourists alike.

A father and daughter fish with cane poles at Ottis's. This was a place where you could relax and talk things over on a peaceful summer afternoon while the charter boats were out.

One

THE WATERFRONT

This 1958 view of the cut on a summer afternoon shows boats returning from a day of fishing from the inlet to the Gulf Stream. The trawler *Edith M.* is docked at the back of Ottis's Fish House. It will leave late in the afternoon to spend a night of trawling for shrimp and return early in the morning to unload its catch.

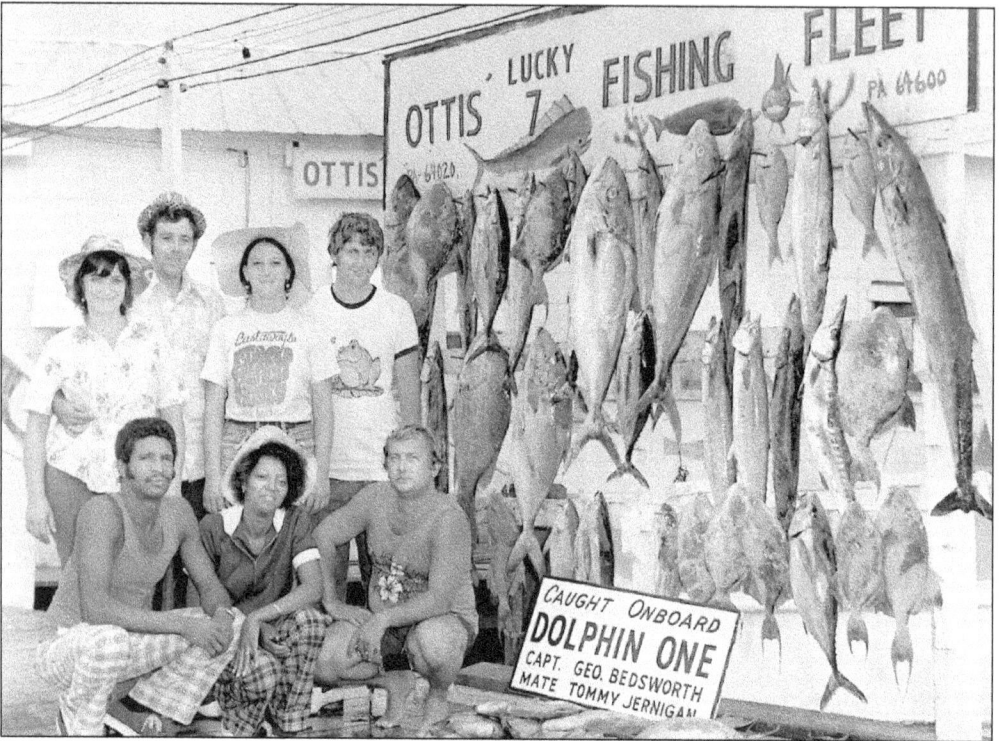

This fishing party shows off a full rack of fish caught on the *Dolphin I* in 1974.

Men at Ottis's Fish House wash off fish before packing them in ice and wooden boxes to be shipped up and down the East Coast in 1955.

10

John Wagner, a local fisherman, is seen cleaning a fish in the late 1950s. He was typical of the old salts along the waterfront.

Little Mary and *Miss Alicia* are seen here at the dock c. 1950. To the right the *Sea Raven* is coming in.

Shrimp trawler *Alpha Gray* is moored at Davis's Fish House Dock, next to Tony's Sanitary Restaurant, sometime in the 1950s.

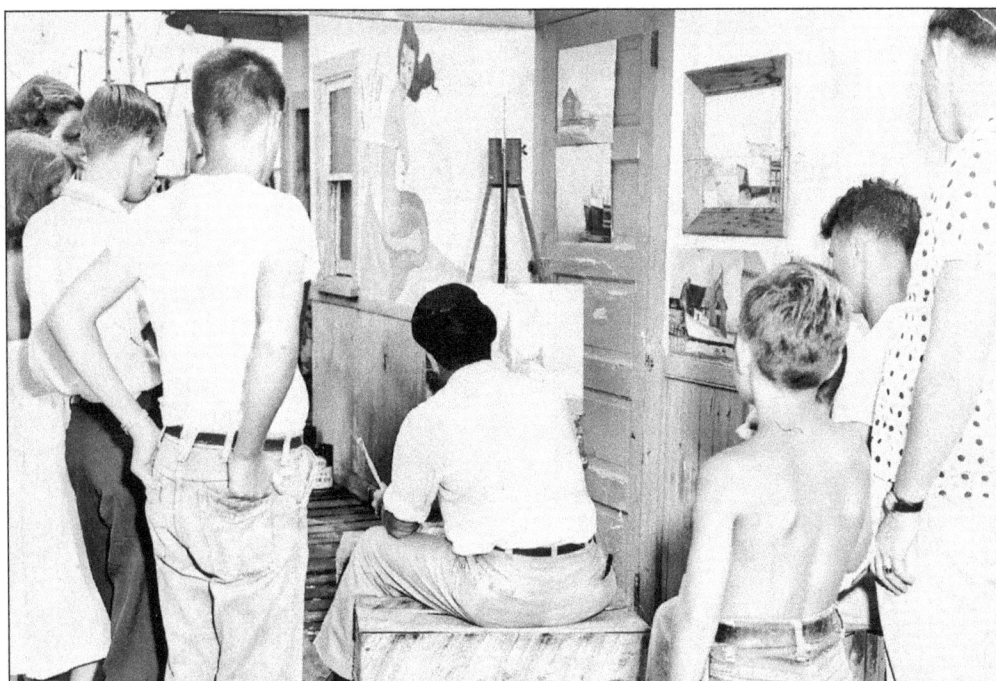

Reginald Lewis, a local and nationally know artist and photographer, is pictured in 1954, doing his favorite thing: painting the waterfront and seascape. He truly loved the people and character of the coast.

This painting by Reginald Lewis is on display inside the fish house in 1959. There were no art galleries on the waterfront at the time. Today there are a number of excellent galleries along the waterfront displaying many works by local artists.

Workers weigh and pack fresh fish in salt. Wooden barrels and wooden buckets packed with fish were sent to various markets up and down the East Coast. These wooden barrels and buckets are no longer used today. Many have become collector's items or, if you are fortunate enough to have one, a great conversation piece.

In the evening, after a shore dinner, families look over the photos on display and some of the items boats have pulled up from the sea floor. This photo was taken in the early 1960s.

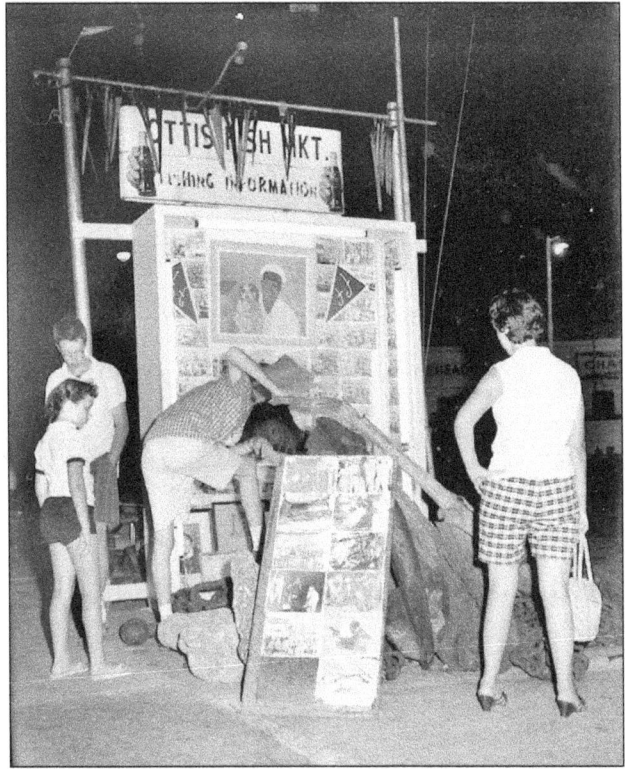

A crowd has gathered in the late 1950s to see what these boats caught while two young boys look on and play on a skiff. Even half sunk, with just a little imagination the boat can take these boys anywhere they wish to go.

Labor Day sailboat races, pictured in 1956, took place in the cut between waterfront and Sugar Loaf Island. Many of these boats were built locally, and are still built by local craftsman today.

The Jefferson Hotel, seen here in 1954, where many fishermen stayed over the years, has been replaced by condominiums.

Jefferson Hotel, Piner's Tugboat, Parker Ford, and the Texaco fuel docks are visible in this 1954 image.

Dick Parker holds a big fish in his Ford dealership showroom in the early 1950s. A local success story, Mr. Parker began by selling candy from the trunk of his car and played a major part in the construction of the Marine Corps airbase at Cherry Point, North Carolina, during World War II before going into the automobile business.

Dick Parker's first showroom was a Chrysler Plymouth dealership on Arendell Street; it backed up to the waterfront.

Elvis the turtle was a well-known attraction at Ottis's. He is seen in this 1954 photo being held by Charlie Wilson.

This photo of the author and his sisters Bonnie and Carol dates from 1956. The picture is representative of many summer afternoons spent with the author's father. It was always an exciting and fun time.

A calm morning on the waterfront is seen in this 1950s photo.

Edith M. *II* is seen here docking after a night trawling for shrimp in the late 1950s.

Fred Royal's barbershop on the waterfront was where many locals got their hair cut. The building was originally a doctor's office before Mr. Royal converted it to a barbershop.

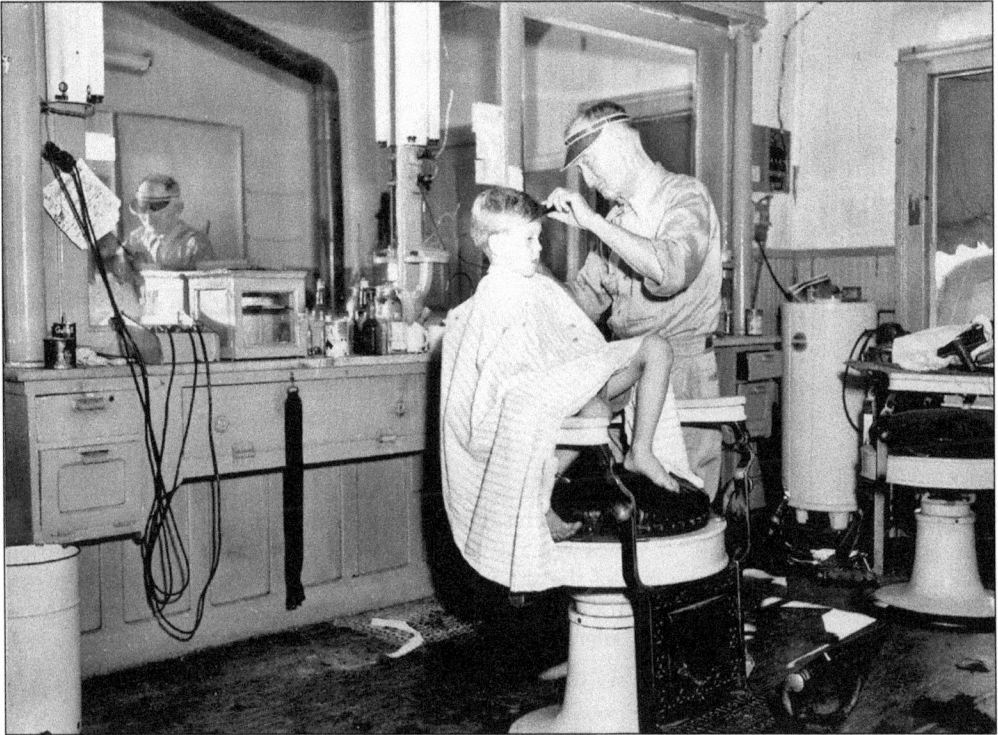
In this 1955 photo we see Fred Royal giving Reg Lewis Jr. his first haircut by a barber.

For many years the Crab Derby was held each summer on the waterfront. The derby drew large crowds and was a fun time for all. Crabs were put in a long wooden shoot with numbers on their backs, and the first one to the end of the shoot was the winner. With Captain Ottis in this 1966 image is Paul Lewis, who won the National Crab Derby in Maryland and Morehead City's derby. For many years this was a popular event up and down the East Coast.

These two photos from the early 1950s are of the Camp Seagull outpost for long cruises and deep-sea fishing. The building in the photo—used as barracks when the campers arrived for their trips—is still used today. The docks and boats in the lower photo have been replaced with private boats and structures.

Chill Wills, a well-known
television and movie actor,
talks with Captain Ottis in
front of Ottis's Fish House while
on a visit to the waterfront.
In the lower image, taken at
Captain Bill's Restaurant
after a shore dinner, Wills is
seen giving an autographed
picture to Tommy Wade.
Mr. Wills, who had worked
with many of the top actors
and actresses of the day, was
always willing to take time with
people, and he was someone you
couldn't help but like.

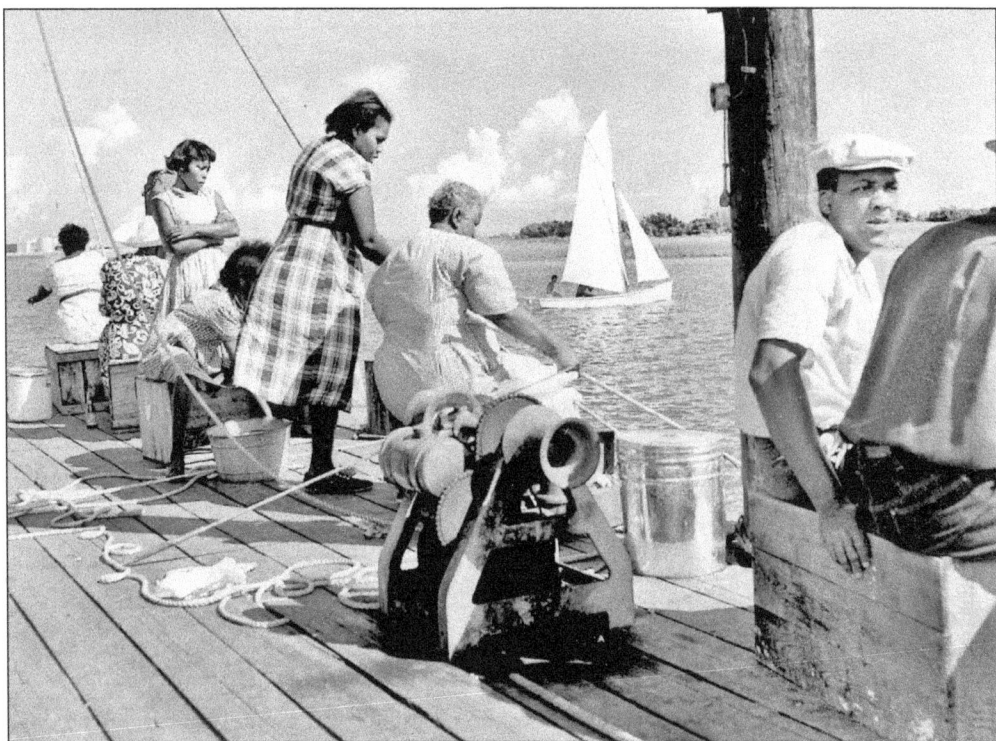

Local residents are seen fishing from Ottis's back dock in 1957. This was a relaxing pastime for many.

This 1958 photo shows Ottis's Fish House and three of his charter boats—the *Dolphin II*, *Sheerwater*, and *Raven*—which belong to the Lucky Seven fishing fleet.

This photo from the early 1950s really shows the character of the waterfront from the cane poles, crab net, man in the door, to the mermaid on the wall. It was a much simpler time.

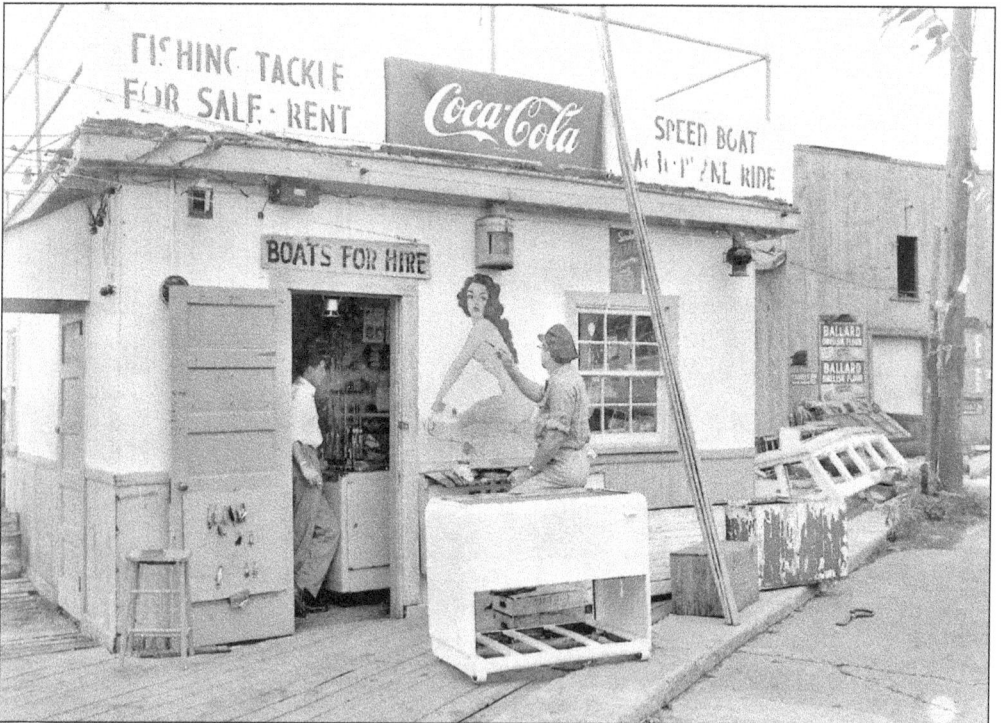

Reginald Lewis is seen here painting a mermaid on the wall in the 1950s. This created a stir with some people. To the right is the old Coca-Cola building.

The Gulf fuel docks are shown here in the late 1940s with boats filling their tanks; this was always a busy place, with vessels traveling north and south on the Intra Coastal Waterway.

This early 1950s image was taken on the Gulf dock looking east to the Texaco docks. The Morehead City water tower, ice and coal plants, and the party boats at berth are all visible.

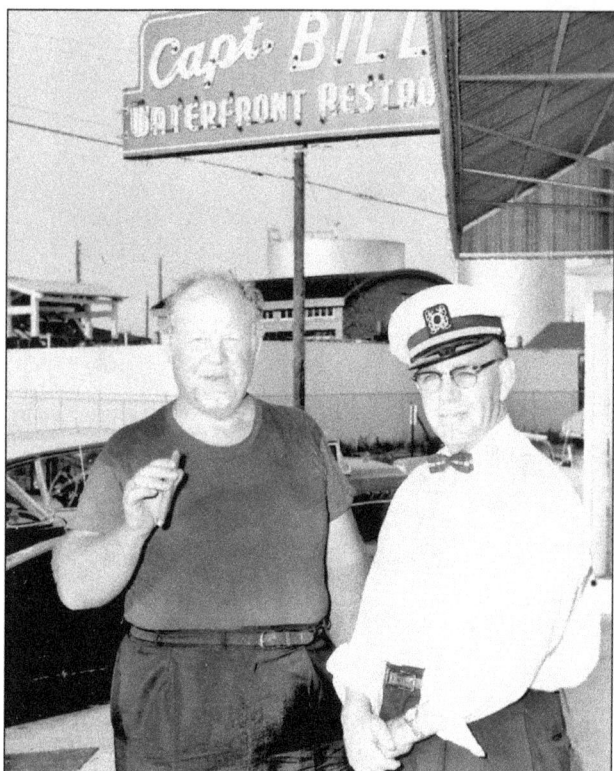

Burl Ives with is seen here with Captain Bill, founder of Captain Bill's Restaurant, after docking his sailboat and enjoying a shore dinner and cigar. In the lower image Mr. Ives is steering his boat while sailing in the cut with the Morehead City port in the background. Mr. Ives was a famous folk singer and actor who began by roaming the country, literally singing for his supper. He gave concerts all over the world and became noted on radio, which led him into motion pictures. He worked with many of Hollywood's most famous stars. He visited this area numerous times while sailing up and down the East Coast.

Boats of Capt. Oliver Davis and the Davis Fish Co. wait for their next trip in this 1970s image.

Purcell Jones (right) and an unidentified friend display a large catch of flounder being sold to Captain Bill's Restaurant in this 1962 image. Mr. Jones was well known in the area. He owned and operated Camp Morehead, a nationally known summer camp for kids. In the background is the Gulf Oil Company and its fuel tanks. Today the fuel storage tanks are gone, and the brick building has been turned into a restaurant.

Rocky Marciano was the only world heavyweight-boxing champion to retire undefeated. He was considered one of the hardest punchers in boxing history. Marciano is pictured above with Thomas Wade, his son, and many locals. Mr. Wade was part owner of Captain Bill's Restaurant at the time. Pictured below is Tony Seaman, founder and owner of Sanitary Restaurant and Fish Market.

This seaplane was used for fish spotting. It is landing in the cut on the waterfront in this 1958 picture; today this is not allowed, and only the North Carolina Marine Fisheries uses a seaplane.

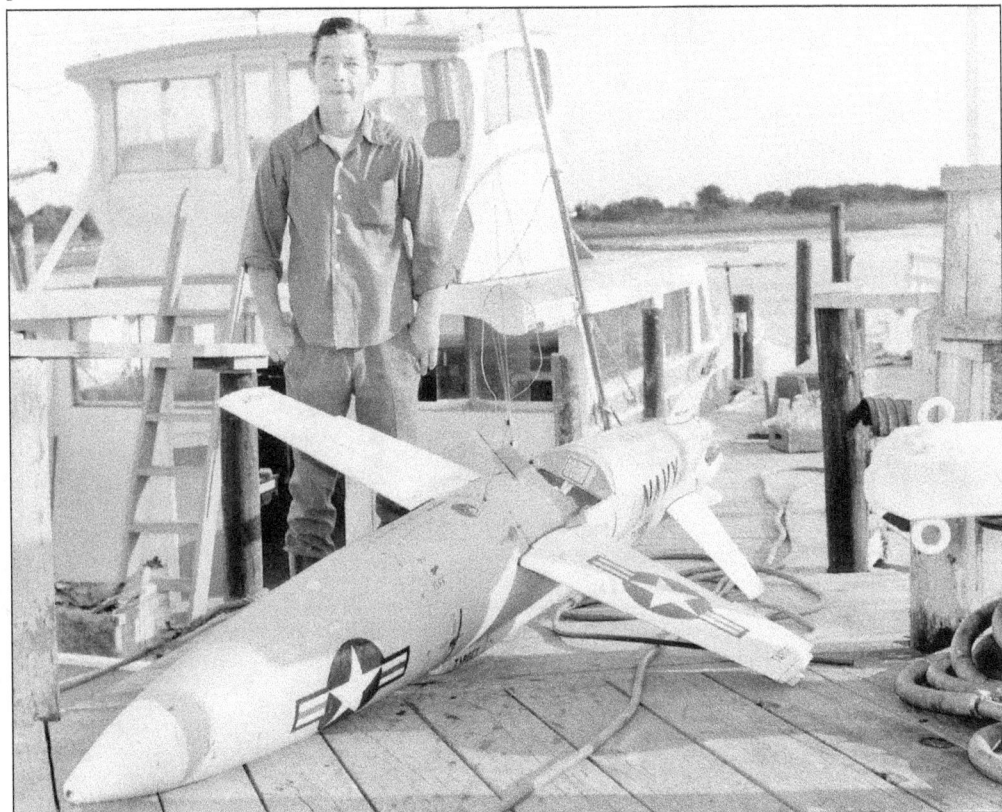

You never know what you may catch—this drone was picked up in the ocean in 1970 on a fishing trip offshore.

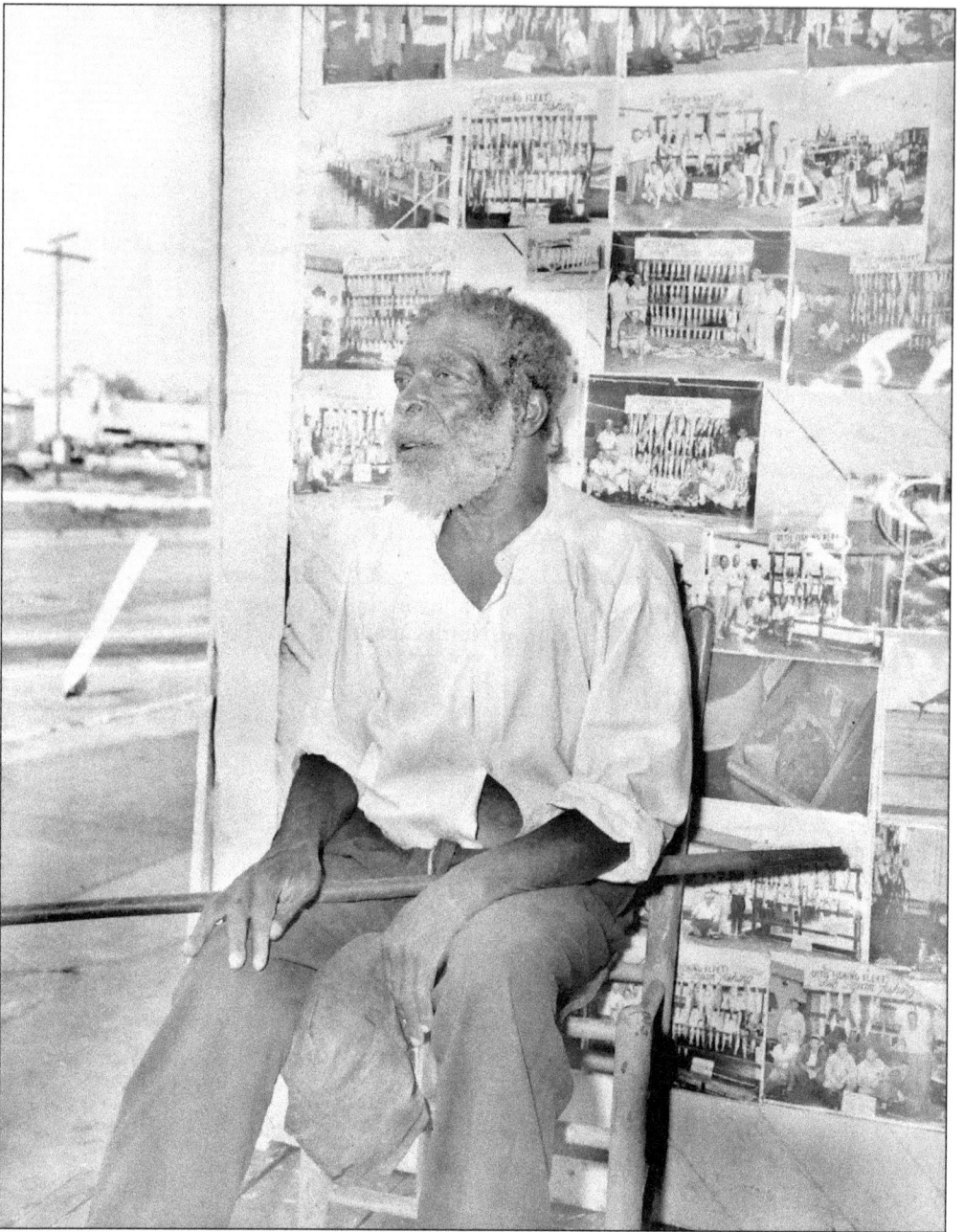

This gentleman rests after a day's work on the waterfront in the early 1950s. He is typical of many who make their living on the waterfront.

Captain Ottis and Mr. William Perry using a band saw to cut this large dolphin into steaks that make for great eating. The picture dates from the early 1950s.

The author is seen here at work on the waterfront when he was 12 years old. This was typical of many young people who worked on the waterfront before regulations were created prohibiting children under 15 to work in these types of jobs.

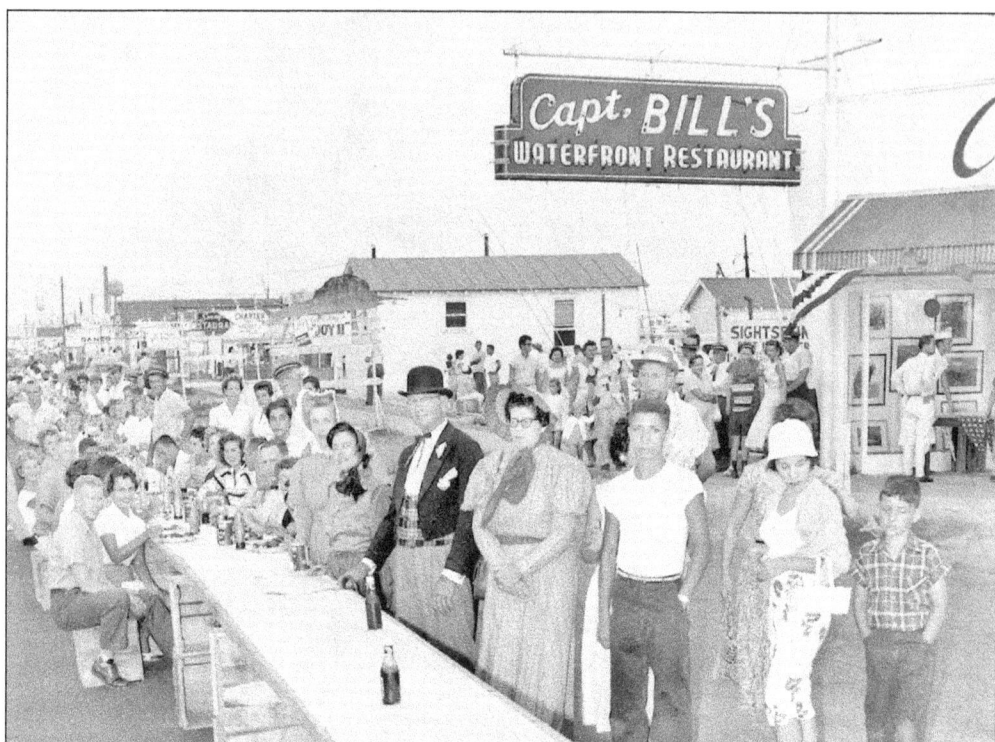

The Morehead Centennial Celebration took place in 1957 on the waterfront. Fish fries, parades, and other festive activities were held.

Centennial sailboat races were run at the west end of Sugar Loaf Island. Large crowds watched the races from docks, menhaden boats, and party boats, c. 1957. Menhaden is a type of fish caught for its oil, used for cat food and other items. These boats were large trawlers, some built just for catching menhaden, and others were converted World War I and World War II U.S. Navy minesweepers. Menhaden was a very large business here from the 1930s through the 1960s. There were at least nine menhaden plants here at one time, while only one is left today in Beaufort.

This picture shows the Centennial Parade that took place on waterfront in 1957.

Centennial fireworks were shot off from Sugar Loaf Island across from the waterfront c. 1957. The island caught on fire from the fireworks. This has occurred many times over the years on the 4th of July.

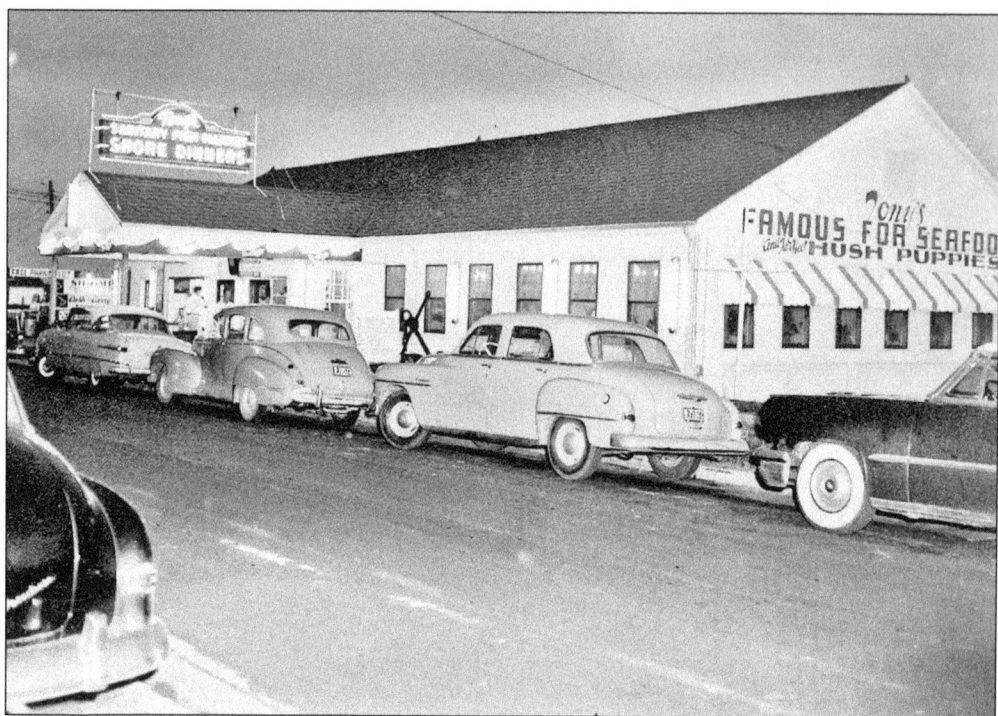

Tony's Sanitary Restaurant and Fish Market is seen as it was in 1952. The restaurant's famous shore dinners have made it one of the top restaurants on the East Coast. You could not beat the price of a shore dinner, as the two young marine officers and their wives learned in the picture below. The food was great and still is today. When on the waterfront the Sanitary is one place you have to visit.

The Sanitary Restaurant and Fish Market, founded by Tony Seaman and Ted Garner, is known all over the world. In these two c. 1952 images, Captain Tony and two employees are catching crabs off the restaurant's dock using a line, bait, and a crab net. Captain Tony is sorting the crabs to be served that day by size.

"The Whittler's Bench" was a place where the old-timers could whittle birds and boats or just pass the time and exchange fish tales. Pictured here swapping fish stories are, from left to right, Cliff Willis, unidentified, Seth Hughs, Mick Lewis, Shelly Bell, Ed Willis, Jim Willis, and Percy Harker. The picture dates from 1956.

Pictured here are locals heading shrimp from the night's catch in the late 1940s. This was a way to earn a few extra dollars for kids and adults. On the right a young man is going to weigh his work; workers were paid by the pound.

Not much has changed—shrimp are still headed, sorted, and weighed the same today. This group of men is pictured at Ottis's in the mid-1950s.

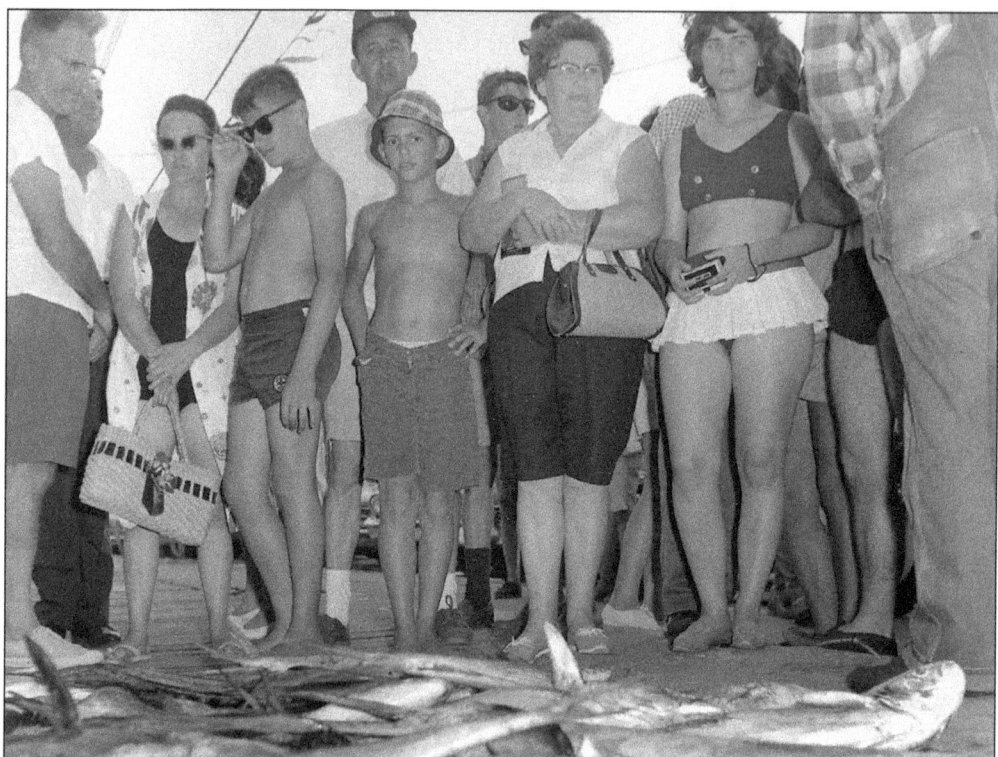

A crowd has gathered to view a fish catch in the mid-1960s. This was a favorite pastime for many.

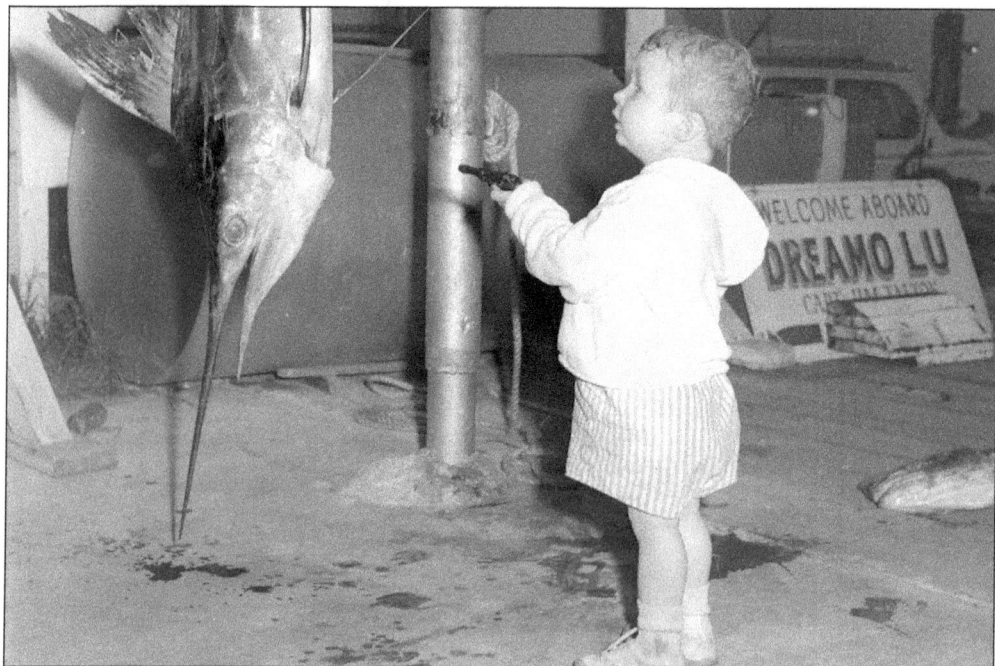

This young man, pictured in the mid-1960s, is telling a sailfish "You may have a sword but I have a gun."

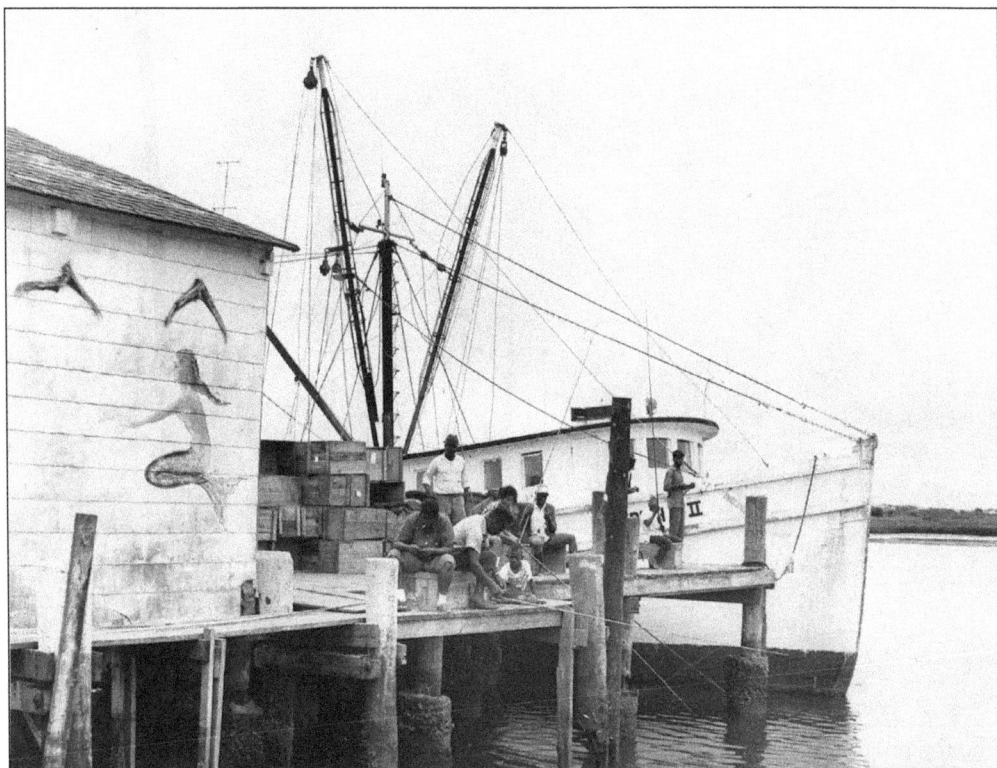

Local men, women, and children are seen in this 1958 photo fishing on Ottis's back dock using cane poles. This was a fun activity—and provided supper as well.

After a hard day's work in the fish house and on the boats, Francis and Tommy Swanson, Roger Grimson, and Junior Bedsworth relax and enjoy the moment in this 1950s photograph. Notice photos on the door showcasing previous parties and events. Captain Ottis was always proud to display these photos for all to see and enjoy.

The top photo was taken in the winter of 2003 after a light snow. The lower photo was taken in 1951 from approximately the same location. In 1951, the fishing information building was located where the lighthouse is today.

Two

THE BOATS

The *Edith* M. was one of the most recognized shrimp trawlers on the waterfront for about 40 years. This photo in 1970 was taken while she was being painted and fitted at Russell's Boat Work on the east end of the waterfront.

The *Dolphin I* was part of Ottis's Lucy Seven fishing fleet, seen here in 1965 coming in from a day of fishing. Capt. George Bedsworth, of the *Dolphin I*, was one of the top deep-sea fishing charter-boat captains on the East Coast.

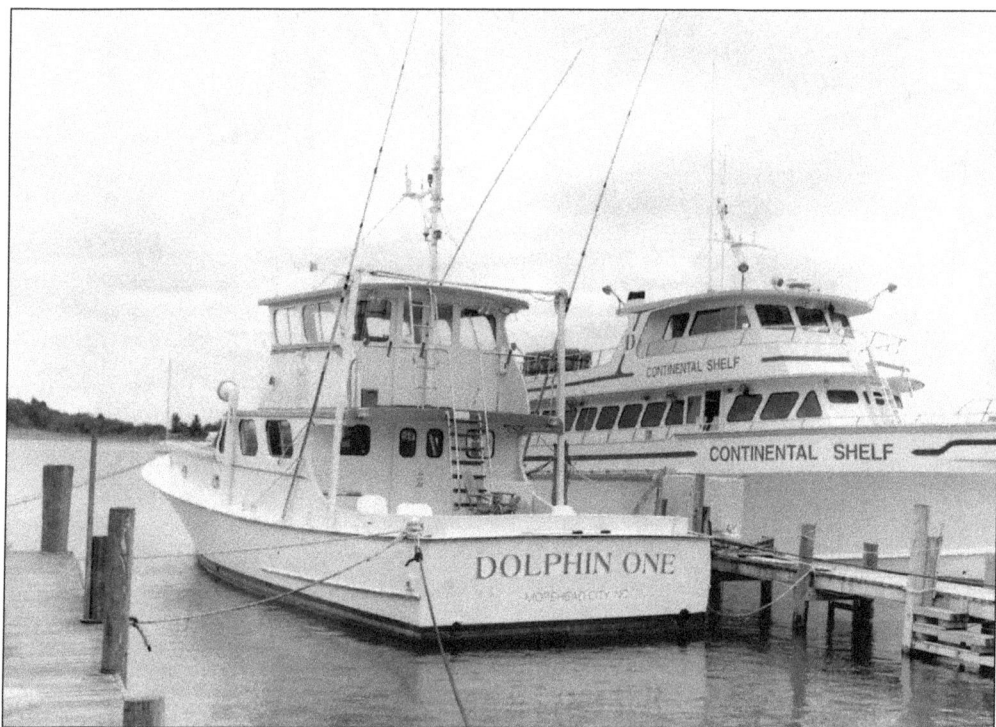

Seen here in 2004 at dock next to the *Continental Shelf*, the *Dolphin I* is still going strong.

The *Blue Water I* was owned and captained by Hubert Fulcher (center), who was chief of police in Morehead City for many years. He was the son of Pappy Joe Fulcher, the oldest living sea captain on the waterfront at the time of this photo, taken in the early 1950s.

The *Dolphin VI* is seen here coming in for the day some time in the 1960s.

The *Little Sister* is pictured here with her party after a trip deep-sea fishing in 1959.

The *Harriet L. II* is seen coming down the cut in 1950.

The *Danco*, a converted World War II PT boat, was purchased by Red Willis, and became the first offshore, bottom-fishing head-boat out of Morehead City. This photo was taken when she was returning from a trip in 1957.

Carolina Princess, one of the early head-boats, is seen in this 1967 photo. A head-boat can take from 40 to 80 or more people fishing out to the Continental Shelf, shipwrecks, or other areas to bottom fish.

Carolina Queen, another early Morehead City head-boat, is pictured here in 1958.

Captain Stacy, pictured here in 1968, was the first in a line with this name.

The shrimp trawler *Little John* is seen at dock in the 1950s.

The *Spanish Main* is pictured here in the 1970s.

The *Caribbean*, a local charter boat, is seen on the waterfront in the 1950s.

The *Gulf Breeze*, part of the Lucky Seven fishing fleet, is pictured in this late-1940s photograph.

Leroy Gould's new boat, the *Mattie G. II*, is shown in 1961 image. Gould was owner and captain.

Capt. John C. Guthrie's boat the *Tommy Lulu* is pictured here, with Morehead's water tower and Carteret Ice and Coal Co. in the background. Today the brick section houses the Ice House Restaurant, and the other section hosts Dee Gee's gift shop and other art galleries.

Miss Heather Anne is seen here in the 1970s, with the *Del Ann* at her stern.

The *Barracuda*, Ottis's first boat, was also the first of the Lucky Seven fishing fleet. The *Barracuda* is in retirement at Jibb Street. It is pictured here in the 1960s.

The *Long Time*, a small wooden shrimp trawler, is seen in this 1982 picture.

The *Lois Ancy II* is pictured going down the cut after a day of deep-sea fishing in the summer of 1970.

Local charter boat, *Am Willis II* is seen here in 1970.

Jeanie II is pictured in 1973 docking on the waterfront.

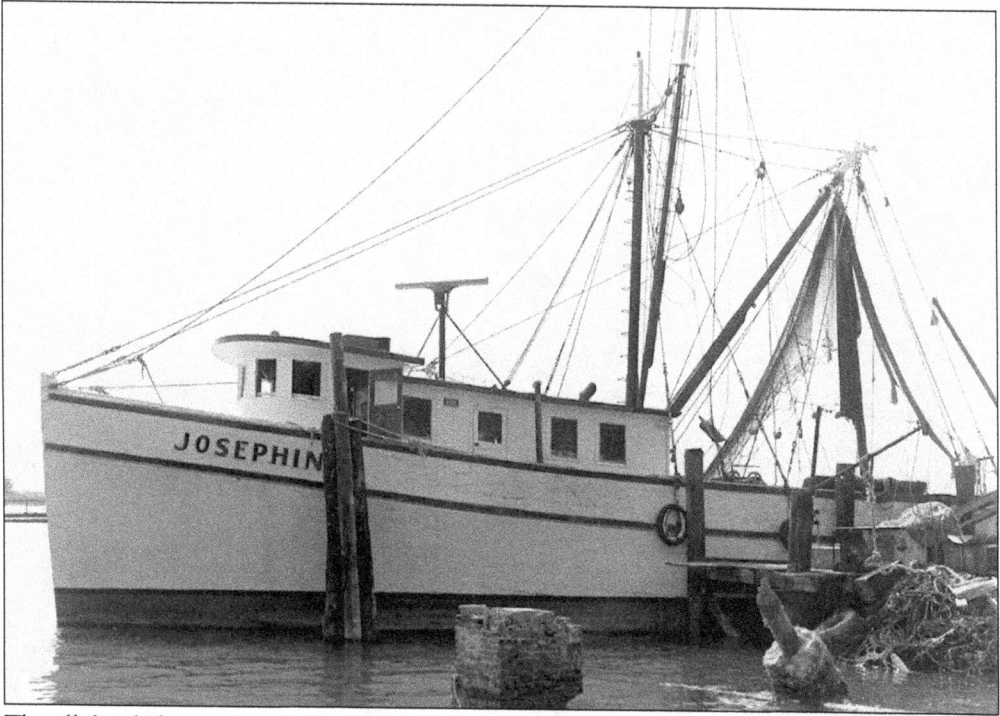

The ill-fated shrimp trawler *Josephine*, seen here in 1970, was lost at sea with all her crew. The loss of the *Josephine* and her crew was a sober reminder of how dangerous a fisherman's life could be.

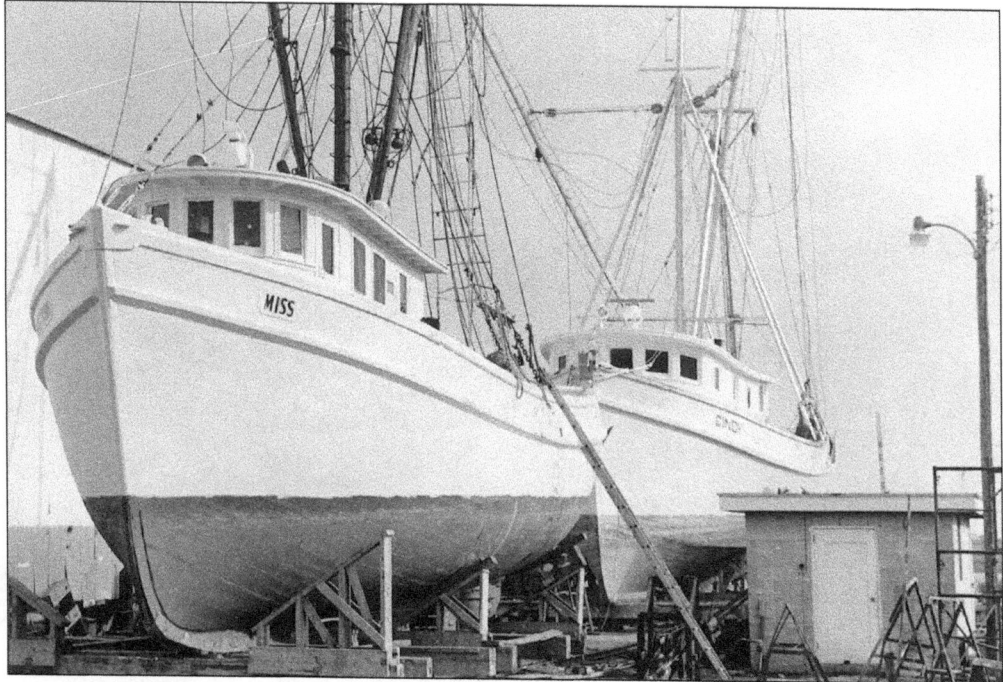

Two wooden shrimp trawlers are shown at Russell's Railways being painted and resealed for another season in the late 1950s. You don't see too many wooden boats today.

The *Bunny Too*, with Capt. Del Willis, is seen at the Gulf fuel docks in 1959. Notice the scuba diver checking out under the hull.

The *C-Oats*, another charter boat that moored on the waterfront for years, is pictured here in 1959.

Three of Puck O'Neal's boats in the late 1940s, the *Diane and Carol*, the *Admiral*, and the *Sea Hawk*, are pictured here. O'Neal was a well-known captain and owner of many fishing boats from this area who fished from Virginia to Florida.

Three local charter boats—the *Mattie G. II*, the *Harriet L. II*, and the *Ebb Tide*—are pictured here in 1959.

The shrimp trawler *Captain Stacy II* is pictured here in 1982.

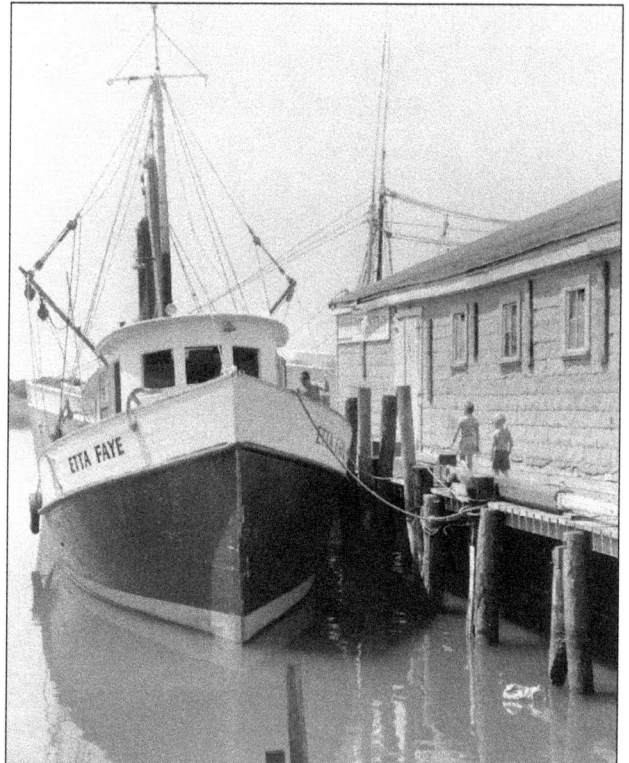

The shrimp trawler *Etta Faye* is pictured at dock on the waterfront in 1956. Two young boys watch another older boy at the bow of the boat at O'Neal's Fish and Oyster Company.

The *Mako* is seen here in 1959; she is still on the waterfront today. The author worked as a mate on this boat for a summer in the 1960s.

The *Sea Raven* is moored at Ottis's in this 1956 image.

Phillip is pictured at Ottis's docks in 1958. This was one of the first of Ottis's boats.

The shrimp trawlers *Hamp Lea* and *Rosalee* are shown here in 1956 at dock on a calm summer morning after a night of trawling for shrimp.

The shrimp trawler *Sherry Ann* sits at rest after a long night trawling for shrimp in this 1966 picture. She was one of Captain Ottis's boats.

The trawler *Alpha Grey* is pictured here at her berth in 1956.

The small trawler *Little Mary* is seen in dry dock in this 1956 photo.

James Howland's charter boat *Bill-N-Jim* is shown here having broken concrete beams replaced at Tommy Russell's dry dock.

Shrimp trawlers *Edith* M. and *Edith* M. *II* are shown here tied up to Ottis's docks next to Captain Bill's Restaurant in 1958.

Various boats are seen tied up to the Gulf fuel docks in 1952. On far left is the *Harriet L.*, next to *Piner's Pilot Boat #1*, which takes the pilot out to guide ships into the port.

Boats of the Lucky Seven fishing fleet are pictured here in the early 1950s. From left to right are the *Dolphin II*, the *Sheerwater*, the *Dolphin I*, and the *Sea Raven*.

Here we see in 1956 the shrimp trawlers *Hemp Lea*, *Rosalee*, *Alpha Grey*, and the stern of the *Little John*. On the opposite dock local residents pass the time fishing with cane poles. Many types of fish were caught off these docks, including hogfish, spots, and others that would make for a quick supper.

Three

THE PORT

The port at Morehead City has been a part of the waterfront from the Civil War and before until now. This image, from the 1970s, shows a young boy looking on as U.S. Navy ship unloads its cargo of marines and their equipment. Troops and equipment for every conflict or war the United States has been involved in from World War I to the present day have left from this port.

This ship, the *Erlangen* of Hamburg, Germany, is berthed at the west end of the port to pick up its cargo of tobacco in the 1970s.

Large wooden containers of tobacco—called "hogs' heads"— are loaded on the *Erlangen* in the 1970s.

A fuel tanker (called an "oiler" in the Navy) is pictured here. The *Esso Charlotte* is seen in the turning basin at the Port Terminal. She was leaking fuel oil and had to make port here to make repairs in the early 1950s.

The German freighter *Bisohfstein* is being pushed into its berth by the tugboat *Manie*, of the Piner Towing and Tug Co. from Morehead City. The *Bisohfstein* would load hogs' heads (large wooden containers of tobacco) to be shipped to Germany. For many years this was a large export product shipped from the port.

The *Marine Chemist* was the first chemical tanker to come to the port of Morehead. These two images were taken in the early 1950s; notice the type of train cars still being used in the lower image. As the port has grown over the years almost every kind of ship and cargo has come and gone from this port. Morehead has one of only two ports of its kind in North Carolina, the other being in Wilmington. These are the only two deep water ports in North Carolina that can handle ships of this size.

The top photo shows the pilot boat *C.H. Piner* moored at the Gulf fuel docks next to Captain Bill's Restaurant. The pilot boat took the harbor pilot out to sea, where he would meet and board ships like the ones in the photo below and guide them safely to port. The harbor pilot was a special person; he was responsible for guiding all ships in and out of the port, and ships could only enter under his direction.

Shown here is an aerial view of the port in the early 1950s. Notice the old Beaufort-Morehead bridge and train trestle. The bridge has been replaced by a modern high-rise bridge so boats can go under and not have to stop for a drawbridge to open any longer. The train trestle has been updated also.

The freighter *North Carolina* enters port in 1950.

The U.S. Navy submarine *Sealion* (SS-315) was in and out of Morehead in 1952. From April to August she operated off the North Carolina and Virginia coasts. The *Sealion*, a *Balco*-class boat, was commissioned in March of 1944 and was named after the first American submarine lost to enemy fire in World War II. She had many combat patrols and earned many battle citations for ships sunk. The *Sealion* was the only American submarine to ever sink an enemy battleship. After the war she was refitted with the LUT hanger at her rear—the big tank in these images. This was added to support UDT (underwater demolition teams), Navy SEALs, and marine recon teams. The *Sealion* ran on diesel engines while surfaced, and when submerged she ran on electric motors.

The USS *Sealion* (SS-315) is shown underway here, leaving the port of Morehead in 1952.

USMC tanks are preparing to be loaded on ships in the 1950s.

USMC M-48 tanks are being loaded onto Navy ships to go overseas early in the 1950s.

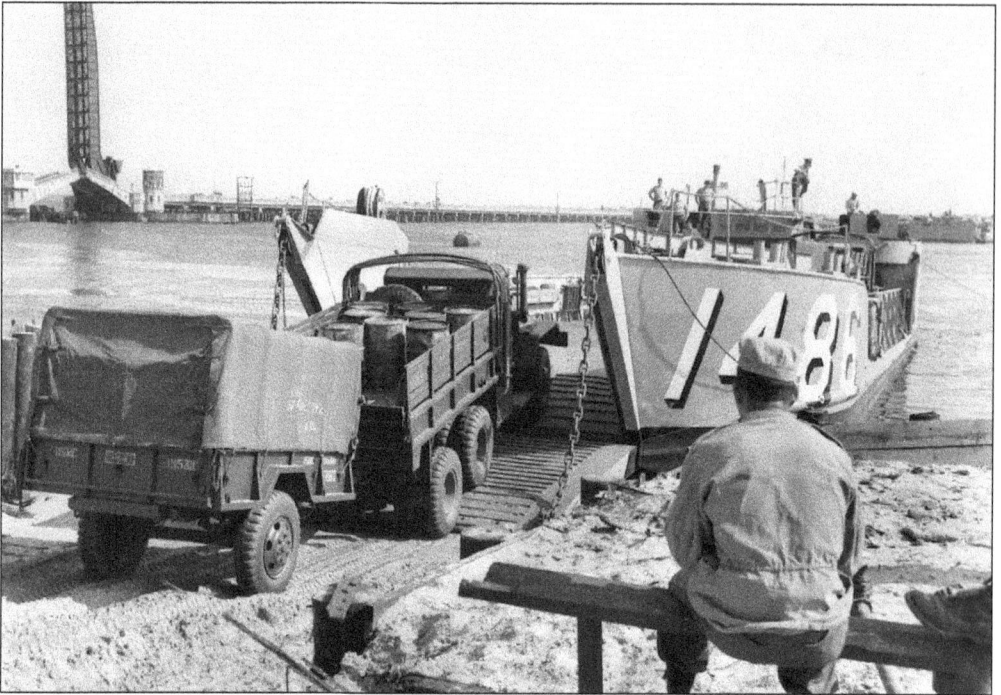

USMC vehicles are being loaded onto navy landing craft in the 1950s. Notice the old Morehead-Beaufort bridge and train trestle in the background.

Military vehicles are being loaded onto landing craft in the 1950s. Notice the silver tanks in the background; they held Asphalt for the Fry Roofing Co. They have been replaced by a wood-chip operation today.

Military vehicles and supplies are being loaded onto navy ships taking men and equipment to places all over the world, c. 1950s.

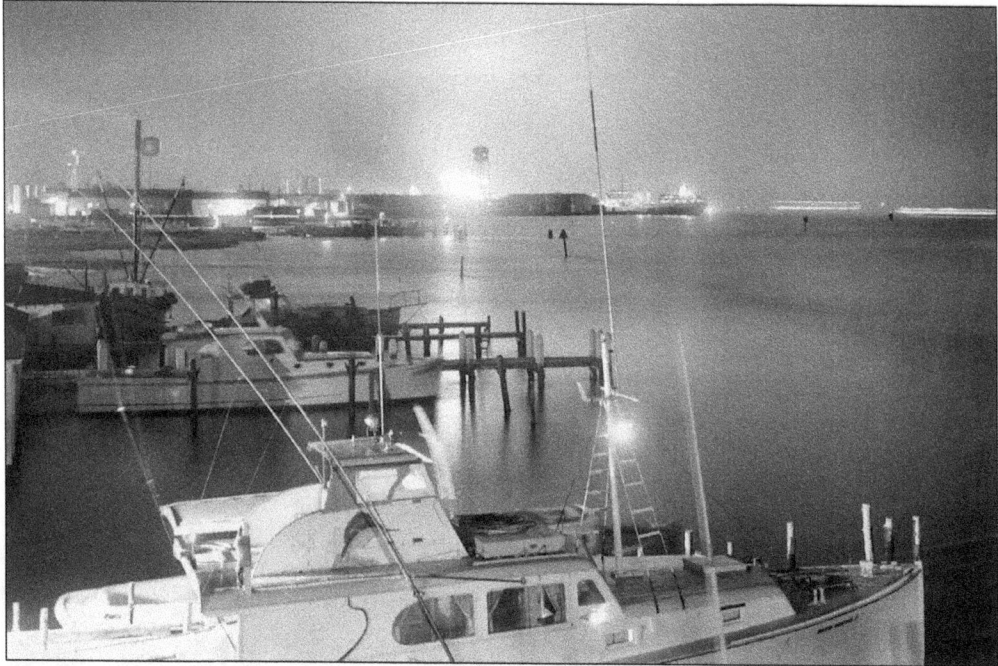

The worst disaster to ever occur at the port happened on September 26, 1960. The USNS *Potomac*, a navy aviation fuel tanker, exploded at the aviation-fuel terminal. No one is sure exactly what caused the disaster, but it is believed fuel was leaking from the line transferring fuel to the tanks on shore. The leaking fuel was carried upriver on the incoming tide and men fishing in a small boat near the tanker accidentally knocked a gas lanterns overboard, igniting the aviation fuel, and like a fuse the fire went to the ship resulting in the explosion.

This image is of the second explosion; notice how the devil's face was captured in this image looking down over the port, c. 1960.

As the ship burns, a helicopter tries to locate survivors c. 1960.

The burning tanker is seen here from charter boats that went out without regard for their own safety to rescue people. There was a great fear the storage tank to the right may explode and cause a large amount of damage to the area.

Local residents look on from Ottis's as the tanker burns. This was the largest disaster then and now to hit the area.

As worries that the fuel tank might explode grew, the National Guard was called in to clear the area. Most of the waterfront was evacuated.

As the fire raged, crews stood by in case they had to move their boats. The crews were transfixed by the burning inferno.

Hours into the fire, it could be seen for miles.

As the aviation fuel spilled over the water, it was feared that the fire would spread to the rest of the port.

This is what the tanker looked like in the light the next day. Only one person was killed and very few were hurt. It was decided to let the fire burn itself out.

After almost two weeks it was over—then began the cleanup. A small boarding party can be seen. Amazingly there was still frozen food in storage areas at the stern (rear) of the ship.

Four

THE FISH

Beth Mayo poses in front of the doors to Ottis's Fish House with two sailfish she caught on September 13, 1958.

Mr. and Mrs. John Adams of Raleigh, North Carolina, and their nephew Buddy Adams of Durham, North Carolina, hold the world-record catch of five blue marlins on the same boat on the same day. They caught the marlins on the *Dolphin I* on June 15, 1959.

Captain Ottis and Frankie Swanson, with other crewmembers, set this marlin up to be photographed on June 15, 1959. Today, with the catch and release program, very few marlin are brought in after being caught.

A marlin is being weighed at the official weighing station for the Blue Marlin Tournament. This station was located in Jibb Street in front of Captain Bill's Restaurant. Over the years they moved around to various locations on the waterfront. This photo was taken in 1982.

These anglers are happy with their catch. The marlin tournament began in 1958 as the Fabulous Fisherman Tournament and has grown to the Big Rock Blue Marlin Tournament of today. Anglers come from all over the world to fish in the tournament and try to win prize money into the millions. It is one of the most respected marlin tournaments in the world today.

You do not come in with a big catch every day—sometimes it is just the fun of trying that counts. Pictured here after a day fishing on the *Danco* in July 1959, are, standing from left to right, John Lewis, Eunice Lewis, Patricia Howland, Mary Ruth Howland, Austin Lewis, and Carol Lewis; David and Jeannie Lewis are sitting in front.

Jimmy Poole of Prince George, Virginia, caught a 151-pound warsaw in August 1972, when he was 14 years old. At that time the fish was world record.

Mr. and Mrs. Charlie Webb of Booneville, North Carolina, caught this rare 54-pound albacore tuna in October 1966.

In the summer of 1956 a mermaid was caught in nets of a fish trawler. After making sure she was not harmed, she was put back into the sea. It is one thing to catch one, but it is bad luck to keep one.

Sally Willis and Douglas Guthrie are pictured here cutting roe out of sea mullets in 1966.

Butch Henderson of Morehead City caught this 440-pound, 10-foot lemon shark in 1976, a record at the time.

Lloyd Reed of Morehead City cleans a large catch of red snapper he caught in October 1956.

Workers are unloading mullet at Ottis's Fish House to be salted and packed for shipment up and down the East Coast for eating and for bait in September 1955. They are being loaded into wooden fish boxes, something you won't see today.

This group of men from Cary, North Carolina, caught this record 120-pound amberjack in November 1977.

LCpl. Larry Cross, USMC, caught this rabbit-fish in the sound in August 1958.

Jim Stroud of Philadelphia caught this record 620-pound sunfish on the boat *Harriett L.* in October 1976.

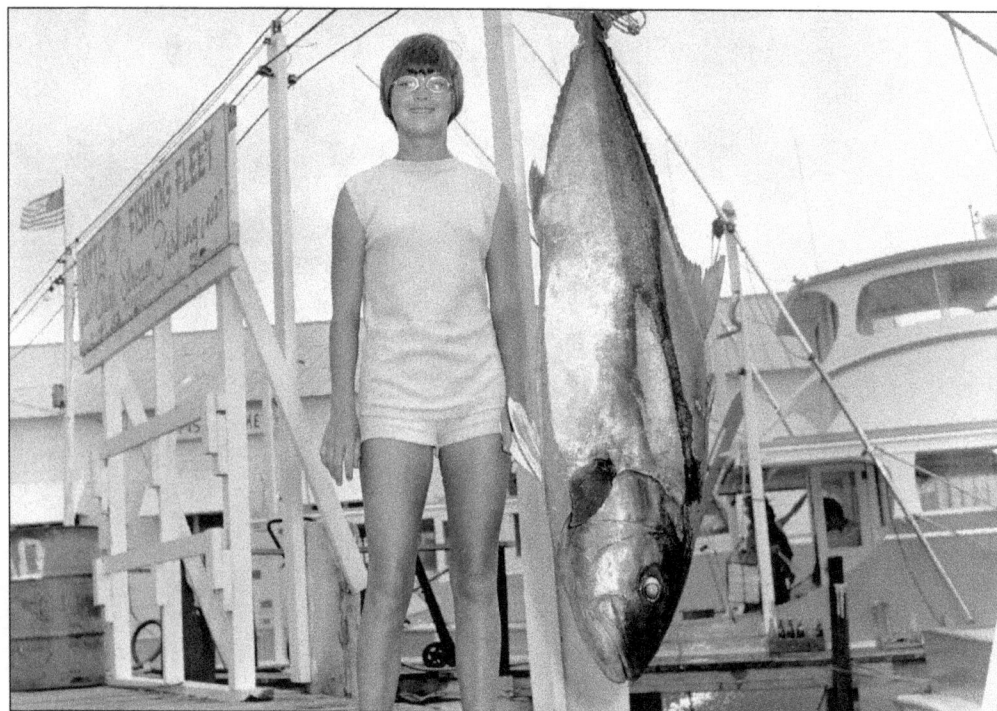

Emily Paulette Cooper, a 15-year-old from Atlantic Beach, North Carolina, caught this record 96-pound amberjack on the *Dolphin I* in June 1971.

Mrs. Vernon Rudolph of
Winston-Salem was the first
woman to catch a blue marlin
here in June 1958.

This large red snapper catch
was made in October 1958.

Steve Garner, 13 years old, caught this record 70-pound, 5-foot–11-inch wahoo aboard the boat *Sam and Dan* in August 1961.

Bryant Guthrie found this rare black pearl while opening clams in June 1957.

Reg Lewis, local artist and photographer, took these images of himself with a time delay, displaying a stone crab he had caught earlier that day. In the lower photo he shows he had a good sense of humor. These crabs are really good, with a large amount of meat. The pictures were taken in August 1954.

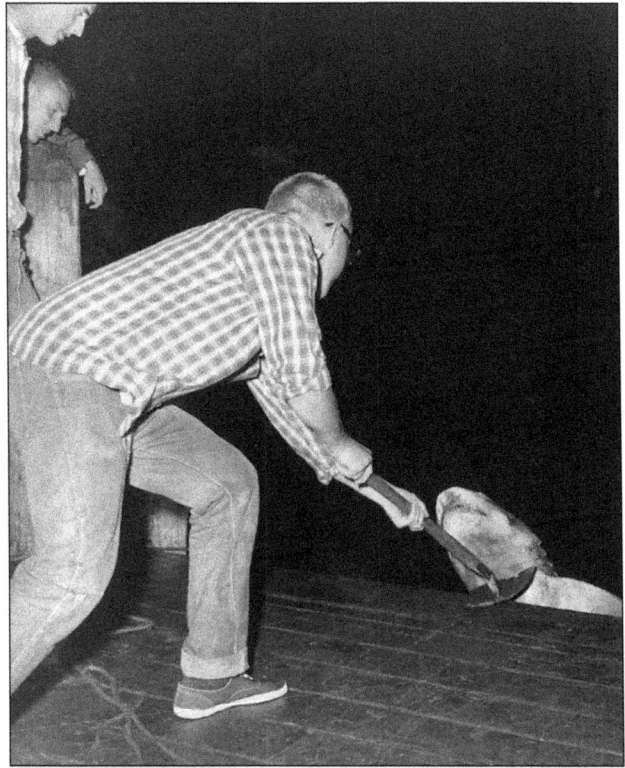

George Whittle, Wayne Cheek, and Ms. Carter McAllister caught this shark off the back dock at Ottis's Fish House. In the 1950s and 1960s it was common practice to go shark fishing along the waterfront behind the fish houses; this is not allowed today. Ms. McAllister is showing the shark's mouth and teeth after getting the hook out. As seen on the following page, the shark is pushed back to live for another day. The photos were taken in July 1957.

This photo shows the shark from the previous page being released.

Paul Norman is pictured here with the 15-pound flounder he gigged near the waterfront in July 1968.

This large sea turtle was caught in the ocean in 1950, and the photo was taken in front of Ottis's. Today it would be unthinkable to catch and keep a turtle of any kind, but back then when you caught a turtle like this one you ate it. The meat is really good, and with cornbread, dumplings, collards, and potatoes, it makes a really good stew.

Pictured here are Frankie Swanson and George Bedsworth next to a great white shark caught on the commercial fishing boat *Alligator* in September 1984. It was over 15 feet long and weighed 2,040 pounds. When the marine biologist from Duke University's marine lab cut it open, he found five sharks of various types in its belly.

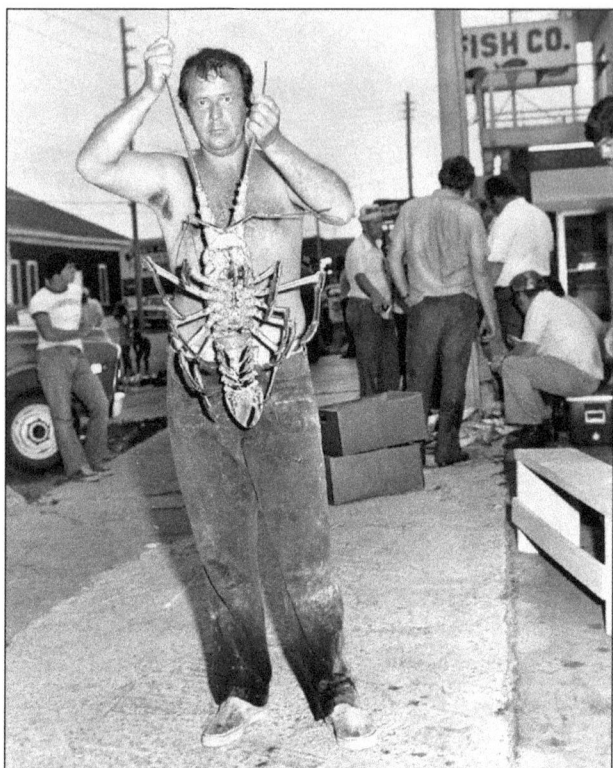

Joe Stabler of the *Captain Stacy* head-boat caught this seven-and-a-half-pound lobster with a hook in June 1974. It is very rare to get a lobster in this area, much less with a hook.

Reginald Willis and his crew, on his boat the *Love Joy*, caught these mullet during a mullet blow in September 1975. A "mullet blow" is when the wind direction would change in the fall of the year and large schools of mullet would head South. Men who normally fished alone would form crews to bring the mullet in with nets.

Five

HURRICANES, LIGHTNING, *and* STORMS

Storm clouds forming over the waterfront make an awesome and all inspiring sight, and one seen frequently on late afternoons during summer. This picture is from 1960.

This photo of a lightning storm over Atlantic Beach was taken from the west end of the waterfront in 1958.

This photo of a lightning storm was taken in the summer of 1960.

This photo of a lightning storm was taken from Ottis's in 1958.

Bolts of lightning arc over the beach in this photo taken from the docks on the waterfront in May 1959.

This lightning storm was captured from the west end of the waterfront in the summer of 1956.

This lightning show over the sound was photographed from Ottis's Fish House in the summer of 1954.

Bolts of lightning are captured from the waterfront lighting up the shrimp trawler *Sherry Ann* during the summer of 1958.

Lightning flashes illuminate the night sky in this 1958 picture.

An electrical storm brightens the sky over the waterfront in 1963.

A powerful bolt of lightning is captured over the sound in this 1959 image.

The west end of the waterfront is pictured here during a hurricane in 1955.

The *Cygne* is tied up next to Captain Bill's waiting for Hurricane Connie to arrive in 1955. This was the calm before the storm.

Two menhaden boats are tied up in front of the hospital waiting for Hurricane Connie in August 1955.

This automobile got stuck in the flood as Hurricane Connie hit in August 1955. The author was living in a small house in the foreground just to the right of the brick building.

This photo was taking in the middle of the Hurricane of 1954.

This photo was also taken during the middle of the Hurricane of 1954. Both restaurants, Captain Bill's and the Sanitary, are still in business.

The deck next to Captain Bill's is shown at the height of the Hurricane of 1956.

A young lady tries to keep her feet dry inside Captain Bill's Restaurant as the building floods in the middle of the storm, c. 1955.

During Hurricane Connie in 1955 this crane was used to stabilize the barge after it broke loose from its moorings in the cut on the waterfront. A large anchor was tethered from the crane and lowered in the water to keep the barge from slamming into the docks on the waterfront and the island across from the waterfront.

The main street of the waterfront and Captain Bill's Restaurant were flooded as a strange calm passed by during the eye of Hurricane Ione in 1956.

These two images were taken from the same location. The top image faces west and lower image faces east in front of Ottis's Fish House at the height of Hurricane Ione in 1956. The water has risen over the seawall flooding the area, and venturing out was very hazardous, as seen in these photos.

This image shows the waterfront on the sound side not long after Hurricane Diane came ashore in 1955.

These men found it easier to take a raft than drive during this hurricane in 1955. The Esso Station was across from Ottis's Fish House, and the life raft was from one of Ottis's charter boats.

Here Captain Ottis and his crew wait out a storm inside the fish house in 1955. As you can see Captain Ottis rolled up his pants legs as the tide rose.

This lady is waiting at the front doors of Ottis's Fish House for Hurricane Donna to pass in 1960.

Six

THE WATERFRONT CAT

The waterfront cat is a special breed—they are not wild, but at the same time they are not tame. Like this one here, they are independent and fun to watch. This photo was taken in the summer of 1958.

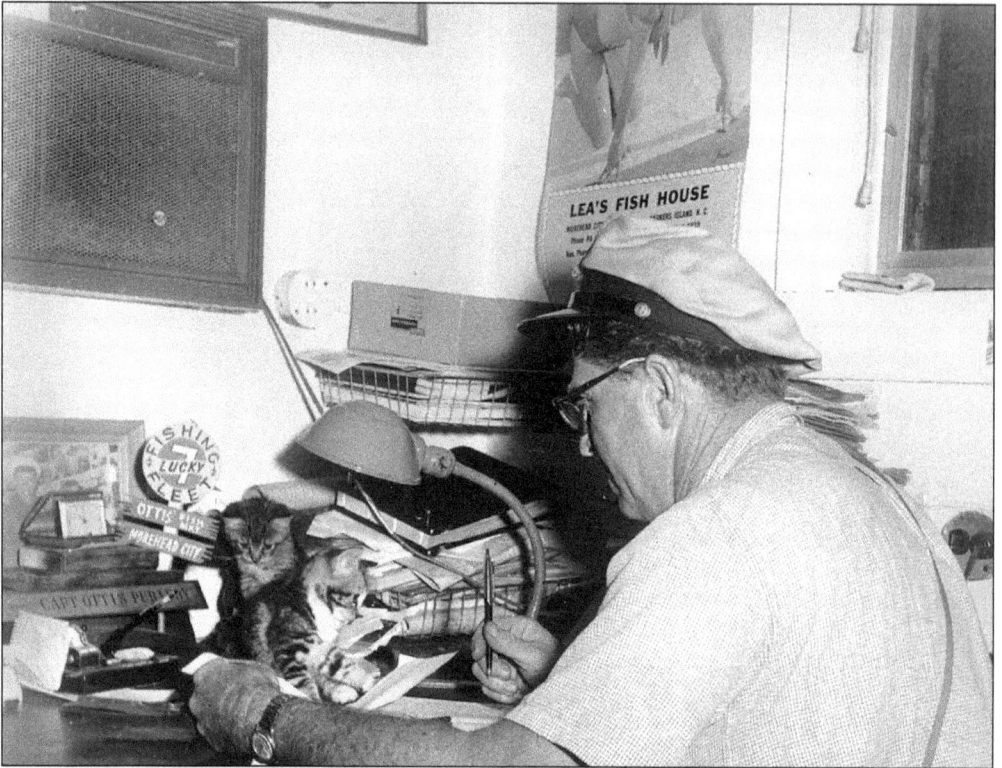

Reg Lewis loved cats and really enjoyed photographing them. Here two kittens are trying to play while he writes. Mr. Lewis was considered one of the top feline photographers in the nation. Many over the years have enjoyed his images of the cats on the waterfront. It is hoped that you will enjoy these images as well.

Captain Ottis really loved his cats too. Here they are going every which way as he has fun with them. This picture dates from 1955.

This photo was taken during a hurricane in 1955. Soap was put on the floor of the fish market and as wind blew it formed soap bubbles, and this cat would go from bubble to bubble, popping each one.

This kitten just woke up, and you can tell by his look he wants to know who drank his Pepsi.

Feeding from a tin pot full of fish scraps stored in the ice bin, this cat enjoys its meal in 1952.

This cat is pictured taking a nap after a meal of fish in 1958.

The waterfront kitten is giving its mother a loving look while another one of its siblings eats dinner in 1974.

A waterfront kitten plays in old nets, driftwood, and other items displayed in front of the fish house that were pulled in by various boats on fishing trips.

Protecting its "catch," this feline was pictured on the Morehead City waterfront in 1962.

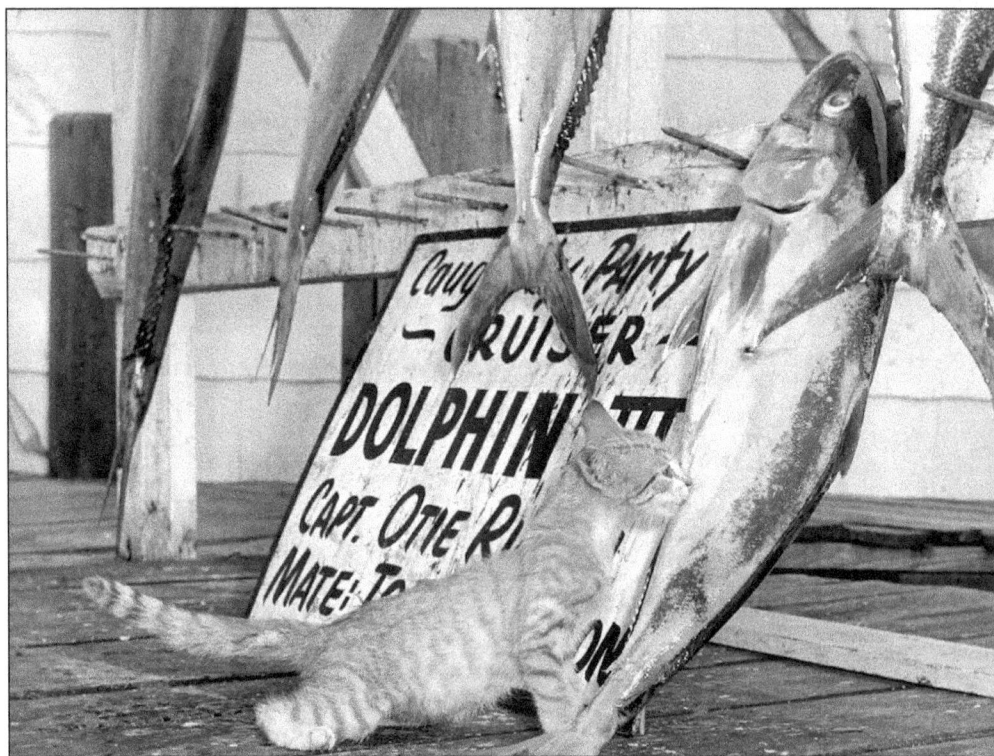

This waterfront cat is having a taste of fish caught that day in 1956.

116

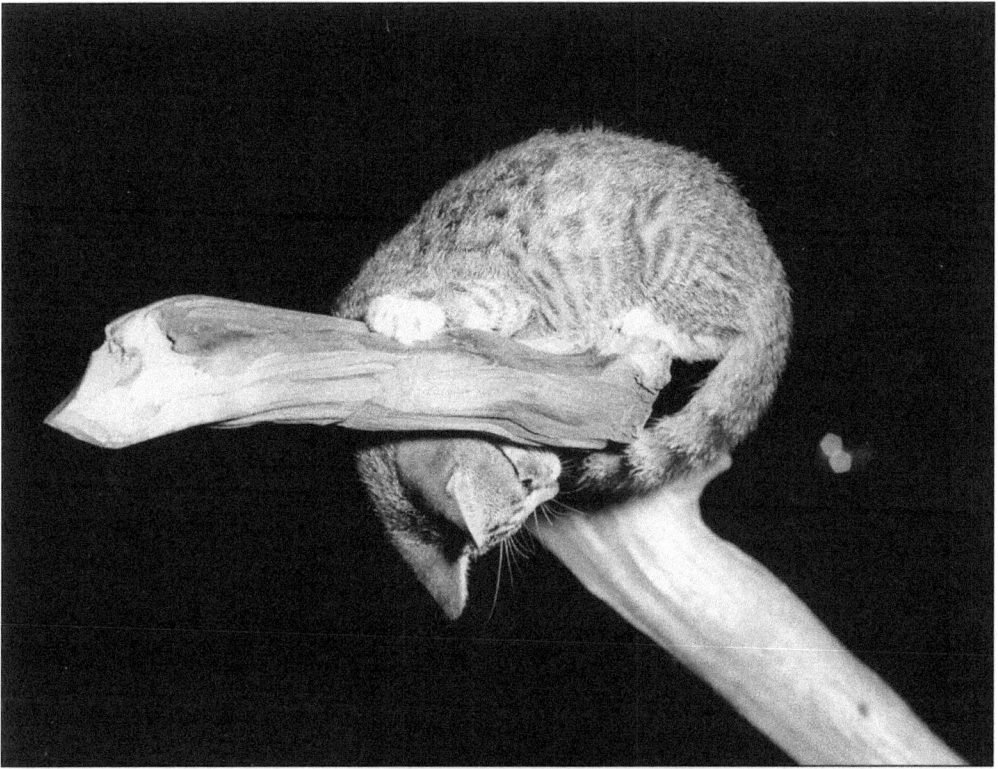

A playful cat chases its tail around a piece of driftwood on the waterfront in 1963.

The feline pictured was caught looking at a photographs of kittens playing and another cat looking at photos in 1965.

The following sequence of photos of this very unusual encounter between a waterfront cat and mouse in front of Ottis's Fish House in July of 1957 was captured by Reg Lewis. In the photo above we see that cat and mouse just staring at each other, waiting to see who will make the first move. Below, the mouse has moved over to an old anchor chain, and the cat is trying to play with it but just can't quite get to it because of the chain.

In these images we see the cat and mouse falling asleep.

After a while they both wake up and the mouse was trying to decide which way to go while the cat looked on.

Finally the mouse decides it's time to go and the cat gives it one last look before they each go their own way.

120

Who said cats can't count? It seems as if this cat is ringing up a sale at the fish market in 1955.

The author is seen here playing with cats at his house at the west end of the waterfront in 1956. There was never a shortage of cats at the waterfront.

This photo was printed in all the major papers in the country on the July 4, 1958. This cat was proud to be an American!

In this image we see a cat and two kittens playing on a wooden fish box—cats were often seen playing on these as they could get their claws into the wood. Today, the fish boxes are no longer made of wood.

122

Three sleepy kittens found a resting spot in the back of this fish house, *c.* 1959.

These four kittens are caught in a heartwarming pose in 1958.

This is an example of the beauty of a waterfront cat.

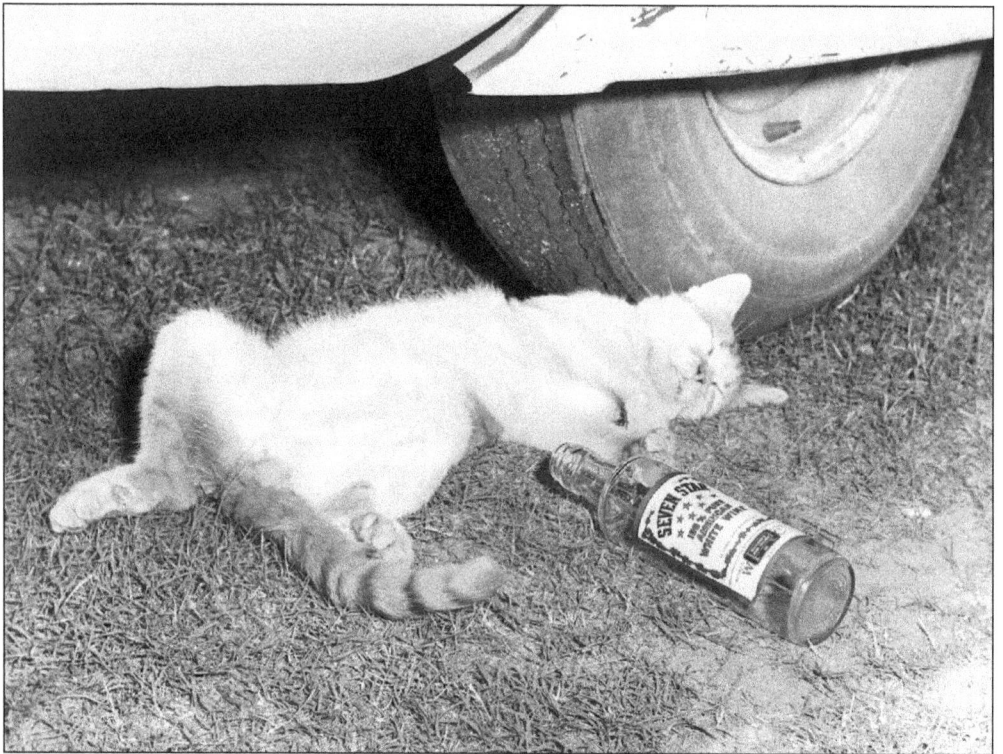

This cat should have stuck to fish. This photo was taken in the summer of 1957.

This feline captured in 1960 is looking over some of the displays at Ottis's Fish House.

This kitten found a spot where no one would bother it and had a good view of everything in the fish house, c. 1970.

This feline was caught behind the camera on a summer night in 1956.

A beautiful waterfront kitten is captured on a summer night playing around items pulled from the sea, which were on display in front of the fish house, c. 1959.

126

This feline is caught in a wide-eyed pose on a summer night in 1959.

A sweet kitten playing around a fish box on the deck of a fish trawler in 1966.

Two kittens resting in a life preserver hang from an old anchor on the waterfront in 1958.

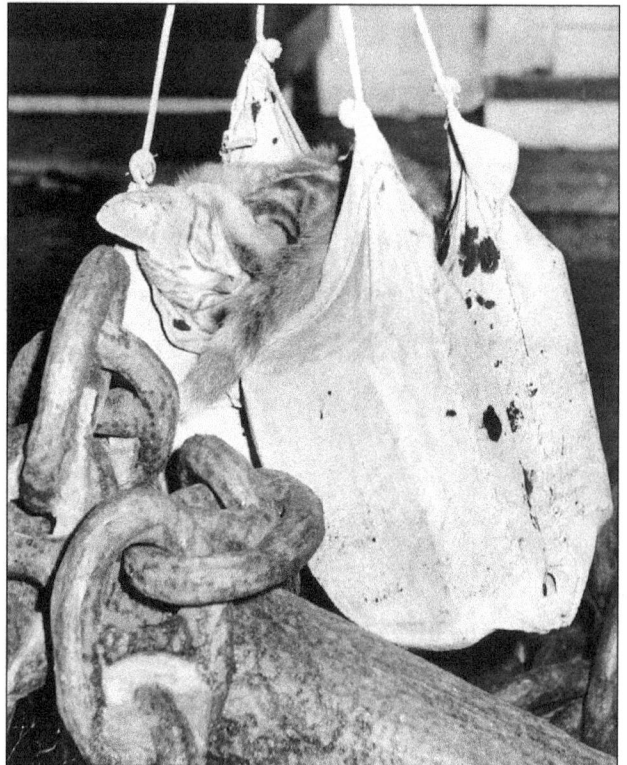

This cat, sleeping in an old life preserver, hangs from an anchor pulled from the bottom of the sea, which was on display in front of the fish house in 1958.

Visit us at
arcadiapublishing.com